Tools for sustainable operation and maintenance of urban infrastructure

Tool 7A and Tool 10

Tools for sustainable operation and maintenance of urban infrastructure

Tool 7A and Tool 10

M. Sohail & A. P. Cotton

Water, Engineering and Development Centre
Loughborough University
2002

Water, Engineering and Development Centre,
Loughborough University,
Leicestershire, LE11 3TU, UK

© WEDC, Loughborough University, 2002

ISBN 13 Paperback: 978 1 84380 016 3
ISBN Ebook: 9781788533621
Book DOI: http://dx.doi.org/10.3362/9781788533621

A catalogue record for this book is available from the British Library.

A reference copy of this publication is also available online at:
http://www.lboro.ac.uk/wedc/publications/

Sohail, M. and Cotton, A.P. (2002)
Tools for sustainable operation and maintenance of urban infrastructure: Tool 7A and Tool 10
WEDC, Loughborough University, UK.

WEDC (The Water, Engineering and Development Centre) at Loughborough University in the UK is one of the world's leading institutions concerned with education, training, research and consultancy for the planning, provision and management of physical infrastructure for development in low- and middleincome countries.

This edition is reprinted and distributed by Practical Action Publishing.
Since 1974, Practical Action Publishing has published and disseminated books and information in support of international development work throughout the world. Practical Action Publishing trades only in support of its parent charity objectives and any profits are covenanted back to Practical Action (Charity Reg. No. 247257, Group VAT Registration No. 880 9924 76).

This document is an output from a project funded by the UK
Department for International Development (DFID)
for the benefit of low-income countries.
The views expressed are not necessarily those of DFID.

Designed at WEDC

Acknowledgements

The authors gratefully acknowledge the many people who have willingly contributed their knowledge, opinion and time to the development of this work.

In particular we wish to thank Mr Micheal Mutter, DFID; Professor Nabeel Hamdi, Oxford Brookes University; Ms Sue Phillips and Dr Ann Condy, Social Development Direct; Mr K A Jayaratne, Mr Kumara and Mr H M U Chularathna, Sevanathe, Colombo, Sri Lanka; Mr N A Watoo, Anjuman-E-Samaji Behbood; Ms Perveen Rehman, Orangi Pilot Project; Mr Norman Ahmed, NED University of Engineering and Technology, Karachi; Professor Arif Hassan, Urban Resources Centre, Karachi; Mr Shahid Mehmood, Community Action Programme, Faisalabad, Pakistan; Centre for Youth and Social Development, Bhubaneswar; Ms Barbara Evans, Water and Sanitation Programme; and WEDC members of staff.

Special thanks to the people from the low-income settlements of case study locations who have contributed to the research and provided their perspectives on the issue. We are greatly indebted to them.

About the Authors

M Sohail is a Senior Research Manager at WEDC and a specialist in project management with special interests in procurement, contracts, urban infrastructure for low-income communities, partnerships, performance improvements and urban public transport. He has recently been involved in undertaking research in Tanzania, Zambia, Pakistan, Sri Lanka, India, South Arica, Argentina, Morocco, Indonesia, and the Philippines.

Andrew Cotton is the Director of Urban Programmes at WEDC and a specialist in the provision of services for urban low-income communities. He is an active member of the Collaborative Council for Water Supply and Sanitation, being Project Manager for the GARNET Global Applied Research Network. He is also an Associate Director of the WELL Resource Centre (Water and Environmental Health at London and Loughborough). His interests include project design, planning and implementation using community-based approaches and municipal management of urban services. He has recently been involved in developing community-based infrastructure projects in several cities in India, and also in Egypt. He earlier worked on similar projects in Pakistan and Sri Lanka.

Contents

List of tables

Background

This document presents the findings from Project R-7397, 'Operation, maintenance and sustainability of services for the urban poor'. The document also indicates a framework for potential community and institutional roles for effective O&M. The purpose of the project is to improve the sustainability of urban services in poor communities by using an appropriate management framework and supporting tools for exteranl agencies, urban government and non-government organisations (NGOs).

The WHO monograph *Tools for assessing the O&M status of water supply and sanitation in developing countries* comprises nine tools which can be used to measure and evaluate the effectiveness of operations and maintenance (O&M) of water supply and sanitation services. These are as follows

Tool 1: Effectiveness of the O&M management system

Tool 2: Guidelines for an audit of O&M

Tool 3: A framework for assessing the status of O&M

Tool 4: Guidelines on O&M performance evaluation

Tool 5: Guidelines on O&M performance reporting

Tool 6: Guidelines for the selection of performance indicators

Tool 7: Performance indicators for water supply and sanitation

Tool 8: Potential information sources

Tool 9: Participatory information-gathering.

Tool 7 suggests performance indicators which are specific to water supply and sanitation; all other tools are generic and apply equally to any other of the urban services. We have therefore provided **Tool 7A** as a supplement to Tool 7 which provides some indicators in relation to these other urban services. However, on looking at Tools 7 and 7A, you will see that it is relatively straightforward to develop 'equivalent' performance indicators yourself for your own use

An additional **Tool 10** has been prepared to offer advice on indicators for technical, financial and institutional sustainability.

Tool 7A

Supplementary tables

The following Tables U7.1A to U7.8 A should be used in placed of the Tables published in the WHO monograph.

Table U7.1A: Users opinions and satisfaction indicators

Indicator	Components or Data	Formula	Application
1. User satisfaction	• User satisfaction surveys	% interviewees satisfied with operation of service classified by degree of satisfaction	All
2. Five main O&M problems	• User satisfaction surveys	% interviewees identifying each of the five most frequently listed problems for urban services provision	All
3. Roles and responsibilities	• Who do the users perceive to be responsible for O&M of urban infrastructure • Who actually carries out O&M work	See note 3 and note 1	All
4. Care and use of facilities	• Evidence of facilities being used and looked after	See note 4	All
5. Approaching formal institutions & outcome	• Number of times formal institutions are approached for assistance in a given period • Number of successful outcomes	Number of successful outcomes divided by number of approaches during the period	Centralised
6. Complaints dealt with	• Number of actions to deal with complaints in a given period • Number of complaints logged in a given period	Number of actions to deal with complaints in a given period divided by Number of complaints logged in a given period	Centralised

Notes on Table U7.1A: Users opinions and satisfaction sndicators

The opinions of the users of services and their level of satisfaction provide essential information about the operation of that service. These indicators are central to the whole concept of evaluating the performance of a service, whether it be managed centrally or by the local community; nevertheless, there has been a surprising reluctance to find out and act on users perceptions. It is important to include the views of the urban poor as well as those in middle and high income areas of cities. There are a number of important indicators in several of the following tables which make use of the user satisfaction survey.

1. User satisfaction surveys are fundamental (see tool 9 on Participatory Information Gathering). In addition to qualitative classification, for example into *'very satisfied, satisfied .... poor* etc, it is possible to explore in detail particular aspects of the service which the users find to be lacking.. In addition, valuable information can be gathered from middle and high income consumers.

2. It is important to maximise the information obtained from user satisfaction surveys through a problem analysis which identifies key areas for action. Tool 9 suggests some lines of enquiry to establish key O&M problems as perceived by the users. See Cotton and Saywell (1998) for details of user perceptions in urban sanitation.

3. This is an important issue for both for centrally managed and community managed systems.

   ■ Institutional responsibilities are often very complex, which contributes to making the complaints procedures long and frustrating. It is therefore very informative to elicit views about where responsibility lies in the eyes of the users. For example, a common response in many cases is that 'the government' is responsible, with no clear picture of the different institutions of 'government'.

   ■ In systems which have tried to establish user involvement in O&M, it is important to establish whether such approaches are understood and are operational in the eyes of the users, or whether they remain theoretical ideas which have not been effectively implemented.

   ■ Use participatory approaches to explore whether caretakers have been identified and how effective they are in the view of the users. This gives a primary indication of whether or not the system is working according to its original concept. Other performance indicators e.g *Functioning Supply points* and *Reliability* can be used to point to the effectiveness of the personnel involved.

4. One of the key user-related issues for O&M is to engender a sense of care and ownership, regardless of whether management is by the household, the community or a central institution. It is common to look for evidence of misuse, for example broken standposts. However, it is important to complement assessments of physical facilities by exploring why this is the case (see Tool 9 on participatory information gathering). There may be evidence of latrines not being used, such as excreta in open drains or on the ground, or being used for other purposes such as storage sheds. This raises fundamental issues about the use and appropriateness of sanitation systems whose implications are much wider than O&M. This is where participatory methods which explore the underlying reasons are particularly useful and powerful.

5. This indicates how responsive the institutions are from the point of view of the user. Note that it is common for representations to be made by intermediaries such as NGOs and local action groups, and also through the local elected political representatives.

6. A system of receiving and acting upon complaints is an essential part of consumer services; utilities, line agencies and municipalities all require a system for receiving and logging complaints. These systems may exist without being well-publicised, and are hence little known to the consumers. For example, whether to complain in writing, or by telephone, or by paying a personal visit to an office. If so, where is the office and what are its opening times? Complaints may be received by locally elected representatives, who keep a formal complaints register. Local community-based management also requires mechanisms for reporting problems; these are much more likely to be verbal and informal. Having received and logged a complaint, the key point is that remedial action is taken. This can be checked by having a simple book-keeping system which allows the action to be recorded against the complaint. The register needs to be subject to external audit on a regular basis.

Table U7.2A: Community and household management indicators

Indicator	Components or Data	Formula	Application
1. Direct work	• Number and description of O&M activities carried out over a given period by community members	Number of activities divided by the duration of the period	Community Household
2. Managed work	• Number and description of O&M activities carried over a given period through engaging third parties	Number of activities divided by the duration of the period	Community Household
3. Financial expenditure	• Total amount spent on operation and repairs carried out both by direct working and by engaging third party over a given period	Total amount divided by the duration of the period	Community Household
4. Labour expenditure	• Total unpaid skilled and unskilled labour days committed to operation and repairs over a given period	Number of days in each category divided by duration of the period	Community Household
5. Problems resolved by internal actions	• Number and description of problems resolved by people themselves over a given period	Number of problems resolved divided by the duration of the period	Community Household

Notes on Table U7.2A: Community and household management indicators

Issues relating to household and community managed systems for urban infrastructure are in general explored using participatory information gathering; whilst important quantitative data can be used to calculate performance indicators, it is important to remember that there is likely to be qualitative data which gives a great deal of insight into what is happening and why. This is very important in developing action plans with user groups and households.

1. This indicates the willingness and capacity of the community to undertake work and, conversely, the extent to which formal institutions are absent.

2. The distinction here relates to the capacity of the community to manage a service rather than just do the work itself. The key point about indicators 1 and 2 is not just that people are actually doing or managing matters related to O&M, but that the awareness of the need to care for facilities exists amongst the users.

3. The financial expenditure indicates the extent and commitment of the users. Note that if this indicator increases regularly, it may also point to major operating deficiencies in the system which need to be rectified.

4. This is interpreted in a similar way to indicator 3, only with contributions made through provision of labour rather than cash. A mixture of these approaches may be adopted; for example, skilled artisans may be contracted in, with unskilled labour being provided by the user groups.

5. It is essential to explore with users and user groups what problems they have resolved; this uncovers deeper explanations of why facilities are functioning satisfactorily and leads to a greater understanding of awareness of O&M issues, the care of facilities, and local capacity for action.

Table U7.3A: Financial indicators

Indicator	Components or Data	Formula	Application
1. Revenue collection efficiency	• Total amount billed for urban services (separately for bills collected through direct user charge and through general municipal taxation) • Total collected (= total tariff revenue)	Total collected divided by total billed	All Managed
2. Billing efficiency	• Total number billed for urban service • Total number of known service connections for that service eligible to pay charges, if applicable	Total billed divided by number of eligible connections	Centralised Community Managed
3. Informal service cost	• Amount paid to Small Scale Enterprises (SSEs) including other households for a given service in a locality	Average amount paid to SSEs divided by local household tariff rate for an equal work or service	Household
4. Operating costs per connection/customer, if applicable	• Total O&M cost for service • Number of connections (include individual and communal)	O&M cost divided by number of connections	Centralised Community Managed
5. Revenue per connection/customers	• Total tariff revenue for service • Number of connections (includes individual and communal)	Tariff revenue divided by number of connections	Centralised Community Managed
6. Cost recovery ratio	• Total O&M costs for service • Total tariff revenue • Total miscellaneous and subsidy income	Total tariff revenue plus subsidies and miscellaneous income divided by total O&M cost	Centralised Community Managed

Notes on Table U7.3 A: Financial indicators

There are many different financial indicators available, and it has been necessary to restrict the listing to those which are likely to be measurable in the context of government bodies whose accounting systems are not geared up to management accounting. In general, up to date financial information is not available in a form for ready use for most Municipalities, and accessing the necessary information can be difficult. Lack of finance and poor cost recovery are major problems. It is important to realise that in addition to financial costs, there are wider economic implications for the poor, relating, for example, to the amount of time required to access basic services.

1. Revenue collection efficiency is one of the most important indicators; many organisations simply do not collect the user charges from those to whom they send bills. Improving this indicator is one of the highest priorities for increasing revenue

2. There are usually many unregistered connections or customers for urban services; the revenue net can be increased by checking up on properties which are identified under the land registration system but which are not registered with the utility. In some municipalities the customer information is outdated and even the bills are not send to many customers.

3. Users who are poorly served by trunk supply may obtain drinking water from formal and informal SSEs (vendors, who include households with their own c connection); the rates may be much higher than the prevailing tariff charged by the utility. However, where other services are procured through SSEs, the point to note is that in many cases the response time may be a lot quicker that from the utility.

4. A major problem in defining an operating cost indicator is that the recorded O&M expenditure does not necessarily reflect the expenditure necessary to operate and maintain the system; the result is a spiralling deterioration of the assets. The problem with the centralised approach is that a budgetary allocation may be made for each household or each community based on the expected income from user charges and subsidies; in other words, whilst 'the books balance', the actual demand for O&M is not met. Asset registers and infrastructure condition surveys are required to determine O&M requirements; until this is done, it may not be appropriate to plan for this indicator to reduce in value.

5. In centralised urban schemes, there are two common ways of collecting revenue. Firstly, through a direct tariff, and secondly through an indirect form of municipal taxation, for example where property tax payments may contain an element of charge for urban services. A community managed system may or may not pay the caretakers, but a maintenance fund will normally be required in order to purchase spare parts, and the contributions in cash or in kind can be explored with the users.

6. It is difficult to extracting information on levels of subsidy in order to calculate meaningful financial indicators for O&M performance.

Table U7.4A: Levels of service indicators

These indicators supplement those for water supply and sanitation provided in Table 7.4 of the WHO monograph

Indicator	Components or Data	Formula	Application
1. Access to functioning, supply points/ latrines/ septic tanks, waste collection points	• Number functioning • Total number in a defined locality	Number functioning divided by total number in the locality	All
2. Cleanliness and visual appearance of public/ shared facilities for solid waste storage	• User satisfaction survey for communal services	% interviewees satisfied with operation classified by degree of satisfaction	Centralised Community managed
3. Location and frequency of flooding in low lying areas	• Frequency (number of times on one year) of flooding to a depth of >150mm standing water for a period of 12 hours or more	Frequency (number of times on one year) of flooding to a depth of >150mm standing water for a period of 12 hours or more	Centralised Community managed
4. Location and frequency of sewer blockages	• Average number of sewer blockages which have to be cleared in a given period	Number of blockages divided by the duration of that period	Centralised
5. Missing or damaged manhole covers	• Number of missing or damaged manhole covers in a locality • Total number of manhole covers	Number of missing or damaged manhole covers in a locality divided by the total number of manhole covers	Centralised
6. Power supply continuity	• Average number of hours per day of supply to a locality over a given period (e.g. number of days)	Average numbers of hours of supply per day divided by 24	Centralised
7. Power supply reliability	• Functioning time: the number of days in a month or year when the power supply is functioning	Functioning time during a particular period divided by the duration of that period	Centralised
8. Power voltage rating	• Voltage at the end of the supply line • Design voltage	Voltage at the end of the supply line divided by the design voltage	Centralised

Notes on Table U7.4A: Levels of service indicators

Levels of service are of great importance to users; they will relate the perceived benefits of the level of service they receive to the cost they have to pay. An overall picture needs to be built up both from objective assessments of performance and from the opinions of users. Note that this table gives some further examples; you will see that it is relatively straightforward to develop your own performance indicators yourself for your own use using these ideas.

1. Access to an adequate service is a key objective of service provision. Participatory information gathering can identify communal services such as standposts, handpumps and communal latrines which are not working. House hold interviews can explore the functioning of individual septic tanks and latrines and service connections. As well as being direct indicators of the O&M status, these also points to the actual benefits which the service provides because they relate to the proportion of the population utilising the systems.

2. One of the major problems with communal facilities is that they tend not to be clean. This is particularly important for sanitation and solid waste collection points. Cleaning is the probably the single most important aspect of operation.

3. Note that the depth and time quoted here are entirely arbitrary; however, participatory information gathering will reveal that depth and standing time of flood water which is regarded a tolerable in the local context.

4. Sewer blockages can be identified either by sewage flooding out of manholes and/or by problems householders have in flushing their toilets due to the fact that the pipes are full as a result of the blockage.

5. Missing manhole covers present serious operational problems because large quantities of solid materials can enter and block the sewerage system.

6. A characteristic of many urban services is that they are discontinuous, for example, with water or power only being delivered to the consumers for a few hours each day. Information needs to be gathered from users and from bulk supply records which may be available centrally. The problem which arises is how to compute the average number of hours per day supplied; ideally it should be an annual average using data from each day of the year in the different supply zones to account for seasonal variations in supply and consumption. Efforts should be made to obtain a value for at least each month of the year. A high value of the indicator implies good continuity of supply.

7. Reliability reflects the most serious problem for users, namely the lack of availability of services due to breakdown. For networked supply systems there are many different components within the system which may cause failure. Different components will have different reliability; the indicator can be applied to individual components of more complex systems. This enables 'weak points' to be highlighted (see Table 7.7 indicators 1 and 2). The reliability indicator may

also point to problems with the system of reporting, diagnosing and repairing faults.

8. If the voltage of the power supply is too low, it may be insufficient to operate many electrical appliances. Some, such as computing equipment, can be seriously damaged by an unpredictable supply where the voltage fluctuates.

Table U7.5A: Materials indicators

Indicator	Components or Data	Formula	Application
1. Outstanding repairs	• Number of outstanding repairs due to lack of spare parts	Number of outstanding repairs due to lack of spare parts at any given point in time	All
2. Location of spares	• User satisfaction and opinions survey	Travel time and/or distance to nearest place to buy supplies for latrines, taps, sand cement etc	Community managed Household managed
3. Accessibility	• Date on which need for spare part is identified • Date of arrival of spare part at the place where it is required	Time elapsed between identifying the need for the spare and the arrival of the spare where it is required	Centralised Community managed
4. Spare parts use	• Number of spare parts requisitioned for a particular scheme over a particular period	Number of spare parts requisitioned for a particular scheme divided by the duration of the period	Centralised Community managed
5. Delivery time	• Date on which an order is placed with a supplier • Date of receipt of the order	Time elapsed between placing an order with a supplier and receipt of the order	Centralised

Notes on Table U7.5A: Materials indicators

The purchase, delivery and storage of materials is an integral part of the O&M management system, whether it be community managed or centralised, and it should be sub-ject to performance checks.

1. The number of outstanding repairs reflects overall problems with obtaining spare parts. Further analysis using delivery time indicators (see note 5) may help identify possible causes of the problems in centralised systems; user opinions and satisfaction surveys are important tools in identifying problems for household and community managed systems.

2. When establishing community managed systems, or programmes which focus on household level facilities such as on-plot sanitation, it is important to identify suppliers of the most commonly used materials and parts (see note 3).

3. The accessibility indicator reflects the time taken for spares to arrive on site in the right place. Problems in supplying centrally managed systems may need to be explored with the suppliers as well as the institution concerned; for example, suppliers may experience problems in getting paid.

4. If very few spare parts are used, this suggests that O&M are not being carried out to the extent which is required. For example, Arlosoroff et al (1987) report that for handpump systems the average period between actions necessary to repair breakdowns or correct poor performance is six months. If, for example, a handpump scheme had requisitioned no spare parts in five years, it might reasonably be assumed that it is not fully functional.

5. The delivery time for spare parts is slightly more sophisticated than the number of outstanding orders in that it measures the effectiveness of the materials supply chain to the stores, including the ordering procedure.

Table U7.6A: Personnel indicators

Indicator	Components or Data	Formula	Application
1. Maintenance team indicator	• No. of maintenance team vehicles on the road in a particular week • Total number of vehicles in the fleet	No of vehicles on the road divided by total number of vehicles in the fleet	Centralised
2. Training (community based)	• No of people trained in a particular community disaggregated by skill • No of water supply points/latrines in that community	No of people trained in a particular community divided by the number of supply points/latrines	Community managed Household managed
3. Training (centralised)	• No of days spent on training per year	No of days spent on training divided by 365	Centralised
4. Idle time	• No of days idle time per month • No of days worked in a particular month	No of days idle time divided by No of days worked in a particular month	Centralised
5. Overtime	• No of days overtime worked per month • No of days worked in a particular month	No of days overtime divided by No of days worked in a particular month	Centralised

Notes on Table U7.6A: Personnel indicators

It is relatively straightforward to develop quantitative indicators in relation to personnel and training; the problem is that they do not necessarily reflect either relevance or quality. As part of programme development, the issue of human resource development should be analysed in detail.

1. If there are centralised mobile maintenance teams, an obvious prerequisite is that they are mobile. The percentage of vehicles on the road gives an indication of the potential effective-ness of mobile maintenance teams. This indicator can also reflect fundamental problems such as lack of fuel. MTBF and MTBR (see Table 7.7, indicators 1&2) are also useful in measuring the performance of vehicle repair and maintenance.

2. Training is an essential component of programmes which are developing community based approaches.

3. The effectiveness of staff within a centralised system depends upon the level of skill and training.

4. Whilst 'shortage of staff' is often quoted anecdotally as a reason for poor O&M performance, it may be that the deployment of existing staff is inefficient. Ashford and Miller (1979) comment on pump operators in Botswana: *"They would be underemployed, in that for long periods each day they would be doing nothing except watching an engine run."*

5. If there are different skill groups employed by centralised systems, for example mechanics and electricians, it may be useful to compute indicators for the whole staff as well as for each of the skill groups. As an illustration, the workload may turn out to be acceptable when averaged over the whole staff; however, this may be the averaged result of, say, an understaffed crew of mechanics and an over staffed crew of electricians.

Table U7.7A: Parts and equipment indicators

Indicator	Components or Data	Formula	Application
1. Mean time to repair (MTTR)	• Number of repairs undertaken in a given period • Total time spent on repairs in that period	Total time spent on repairs divided by number of repairs in the given period	All
2. Mean time before failure (MTBF)	• Number of equipment breakdowns in a system in a given period	Duration of period divided by number of failures in that period	All
3. Leakage repair rate (water supply only)	• Number of leakages repaired in a given period	Number of leakages repaired divided by duration of the period	Centralised
4. Unaccounted for services, such as water	• Total annual production of water • Total annual metered consumption • Non metered water consumption	Total annual production minus total annual metered consumption minus estimated annual non-metered consumption	Centralised

Notes on Table U7.7A: Parts and equipment indicators

Implementing rapid and effective repairs to system components and equipment is an integral part of the O&M management system, whether it be community managed or centralised.

1. The mean time to repair (MTTR) gives an indication of how long it takes to carry out a maintenance job and reflects the reliability of the system. Low MTTR points to systems which are easy to maintain and to efficiently organised maintenance work. The MTTR measures the 'maintainability' of a system. It also reflects the efficiency of the work control system (see Table 7.8)

2. Another common measure of the reliability of a mechanical system is the mean time between failure (MTBF). This is the length of time for which the system can be expected to operate before some maintenance input is required to rectify problems which have caused the system to breakdown. The higher this MTBF, the less frequently breakdowns occur and the better the performance. A low MTBF may point to bad maintenance or to poor equipment condition due to excessive wear. Both MTBF and MTBR can be most usefully applied to particular items of equipment such as vehicles and handpumps.

3. Note that MTTR and MTBF are not the same as the reliability indicator (see Table 7.4 Indicator 3). Reliability relates to the actual time the system functions, whereas MTTR and MTBF do not necessarily take account of the lead time between reporting a fault and arriving to fix it. The difference between MTTR and MTBF can be illustrated by this example.

The water supply to Settlement 'A' has a surface water source with a stream intake structure which silts up during the rainy season.
The MTBF is 6 months and the MTTR is 1 week.
The water supply to Settlement 'B' is using handpumps.
The MTBF is 20 months and the MTTR is 1.5 months.
In terms of MTBF, settlement 'B' is judged to have a better supply than village 'A'.
However, in terms of reliability as defined above
Reliability for settlement 'A' = 26/27x 100 = 96%
Reliability for settlement 'B' = 20/21.5 x 100= 93%
Therefore according to the reliability indicator, settlement 'A' has a more reliable water supply.

4. The leakage repair rate is relatively easy to measure compared with unac counted for water, and is an important indicator in the early stages of efforts to improve water distribution systems.

Table U7.8A: Work control indicators

Indicator	Components or Data	Formula	Application
1. Work Control Indicator	• Number of outstanding jobs unfinished (the backlog)	Number of outstanding jobs unfinished at any point in time	Centralised
2. Workload	• Number of jobs carried out classified by type over a particular period	Number of jobs carried out in each classification divided by the duration of the period	Centralised

Notes on Table U7.8 A: Work control indicators

Effective control of work is essential to avoid unnecessary delays in responding to breakdowns.

As well as highlighting current difficulties, the backlog provides advance warning of problems with future workload; continual high levels of backlog indicate systemic problems for which the system needs to be reviewed and improved. This indicator could be refined by considering different categories of work. Poor performance in general may also point to factors which are more far reaching. The number of visits to site which are required to effect a repair is likely to be a function of the skill and competence of the workers.

For the workload indicator it is best to classify the work; for example: handpumps; standposts; latrines; pipelines; fittings; other equipment; vehicles; buildings.

Tool 10

Tool 10 – Sustainability indicators; technical, financial and institutional.
Table10.1: Technical Sustainability Indicators

Indicator	Description
Did the services provided respond to community needs, in general and in terms of their technical specification?	Why: Participatory methods used to identify community needs, ability of community to engage in discussions of technical specifications, government may be unable to provide services for all communities or not in consultation with communities, self help efforts may follow poor technical specifications which increase O&M requirements, Key sources of information: user satisfaction surveys; complaints logbooks, actions to deal with complaints, quality of services, numbers of functioning services, performance indicators (flow rates etc.) How: Number of incidences of responding to community demand. Comments: communities involved in decisions about what kind of services should be provided, the technical design specifications and the implications for O&M
What kinds of O&M were required for the different community services?	Why NGOs may be providing social and technical guidance and tools and supervision for communities – community can acquire skills for O&M. Local government staff may have the expertise to conduct O&M but lack the resources to do the work and lack the resources to engage in public awareness campaigns to prevent misuse of facilities (e.g. blocking sewers) Key sources of information: key informants surveys, documentation, work logbooks. How: Listing of categories of O&M activities Comments: Support to community is crucial.
What level of technical expertise was required for different levels of O&M?	Why: Municipal workers may lack the knowledge of how the system works and thus aggravate O&M requirements. Community members may receive some training in O&M from NGOs and thus acquire the necessary skills and expertise themselves Key sources of information: number of days spent on training, number of people trained in a particular skill, key informant interviews, number of functioning services/ continuity of services. How: Skill profile of the community Comments: Not all communities are same for the availability of skill. In mist urban settlement some sort of basic skill may be available but may need further training
Were the necessary skills and resources available to staff to carry out O&M?	Why: O&M may be constrained by resources available and capacity of the staff/ community Key sources of information: financial reporting and information systems; stock records, documentation in relation to spares etc., How: Skill profile of the community, number of training days including on the job trainging. Comments: finance, personnel, repair for facilities, material, information and documentation.
How were community needs identified (in consultation with the community)?	Why: Level of O&M needed may increase with inappropriate infrastructure alternatively disinterest may result in community managed O&M.

Composition of maintenance skills (numbers, type of skills/ unskilled labour)	Key sources of information: key informant interviews, user satisfaction surveys. How: Number and quality of community meeting and the power relations in them. Comments: It is not only the number of meeting but also the power dynamics which is important
	Why: Capacity to carry out O&M may be dependent on the workers. Key sources of information: key informant interviews, work logbooks, technical information. How: Number of skill and unskilled worker in the community. Comments: Some sort of skill baseline is important.
Training of staff	Why: skills incentive, capacities, reporting system; financial and technical feedback; attitudes of staff, materials. Key sources of information: training available, days devoted to training each year, capacity of maintenance team, incentives; document review and key informant interviews. How: Number of training days including on the job training and informal training mechanisms. Comments: Distinction between formal and informal training is important.
Job satisfaction	Why: Lack of incentive to carry out O&M tasks. Key sources of information: key informant interviews, work loads, opinion surveys, organisations ethos, perception of roles and responsibilities, incentives/ sanctions. How: Length of service, Satisfaction level, number of complaints and disputes, number of initiatives. Comments: Length of service in an organization should be used with other indicators
Staff Attitude to O&M	Why: O&M may be given low priority in the organisational culture. Key sources of information: key informant interviews, number of outstanding repairs, user satisfaction and opinion surveys. How: Attitude towards O&M staff, number of promotion of related staff correcting for total number of staff. Comments: The status of O&M should be raised in an organization.

Table 10.2: Financial sustainability indicators

Indicator	Description
What policies were established on cost recovery or cost sharing for the services as a whole and O&M in particular?	Why: community member contribute to the cost of small scale O&M whilst for large scale works municipalities take responsibility, community make unofficial payment to workers to get the repairs done; community raises funds for specific repairs. Communities may finance the construction and maintenance of infrastructure. Key sources of information: documents, financial reporting and information systems; book keeping, key informant interviews How: Numbers and scope of relevant polices, evidences implementing those policies. Comments: are local authority funds earmarked and sufficient for O&M, extent to which unofficial payments are made to workers; exceptions made for poorer or more vulnerable groups? Role of cross subsidies?
Were communities consulted on these policies and in relation to the choice of technical options?	Why: communities may be involved in technical drawing and guidance, contribution to the choice of design and system of O&M; communities may be unwilling to raise funds for activities which do not result in new infrastructure, disinterest in O&M Key sources of information: key informant interviews, records How: Number and scope of consultation, incidences of Utilities being influenced by users demand. Comments: establish if communities agreed to proposed cost recovery policy and to investigate the community perception of O&M/ ownership of infrastructure and perceptions of quality / value of service.
Mechanisms put in place for costs to be recovered?	Why: communities may raise money for repairs in the communities, money may only be collected for specific repairs, ability of community to maintain a regular O&M fund, local employment generating opportunities or fund raising from infrastructure Key sources of information: financial records, key informant interviews How: Bills delivered to customers, recovery and follow-ups. Comments: local authority billing may be weak and record keeping poor; effects of disconnections/ other sanctions; political interference; community distrust or perceive the service delivery as unfair. Who recovered costs and how did the system work, how is money accounted for and is this transparent.
Factors affected willingness to pay?	Why: affects the total amount of money available for operation and maintenance Key sources of information: user surveys How: Relative willingness to pay backed by money, changes in willingness under different scenario. Comments: quality and reliability of service, ownership of infrastructure, perceived level of corruption, level of health education etc.
How efficient is the collection of bills	Why: affects the total amount of money available for operation and maintenance. Key sources of information: financial & user records, user surveys, total tariff revenue for services How: Amount recovered/Amount billed at a given time Comments: Effectiveness to be considered as well

How efficient is the billing procedure	Why: affects the number of people who pay their bills Key sources of information: financial and user records, user surveys, total number of people billed for urban services, total number known to be eligible to pay; number of connections to water and sanitation. How: Scope of coverage, proportion of unregistered customers Comments: Effectiveness to be considered as well.
How much do people pay for water for vendors (and the extent of informal water provision)	Why: indication of people outside the formal provision of urban services Key sources of information: records and user surveys, How: Money transaction, coverage by informal sector, variety of mechanisms Comments: For most informal settlement the issue the effectiveness and efficiency of informal sector.
How much are people paying to use public latrines (informal sanitation costs and extent of use)	Why: indication of people outside the formal provision of urban services Key sources of information: records and user surveys How: Tariffs and proxy tariffs for such services Comments: In some cases it is hard to estimate the real cost by the real issue is the how much a customer pay for a given level of service.
How much of the budget of public institutions devoted to O&M (total O&M costs for urban services)	Why: to discover whether O&M is ear marked in the budget, total O&M costs for services and other incomes, estimate cost recovery Key sources of information: financial records, budgets, end of year acoounts. How: Percentage, trends over many years. Comments: Trend are more important than a spot value, five year is a reasonable time period to start with. Finding actual total O&M cost is difficult.

Table 10.3: Institutional sustainability indicators

Indicator	Description
At what stages were communities involved in the infrastructure projects and programmes	Why: Service providers often finance works, yet communities may collaborate in terms of participating in identifying needs, contributing skilled and unskilled labour, collecting money to finance small repairs and manage and supervise construction of infrastructure. Key sources of information: user surveys, key informant interviews How: Number of community meetings at different stages of the project in relation to O&M. Comments: Non participation may have consequences for use of services i.e. throwing rubbish in drains. This behaviour may stem from lack of participation in setting performance standards i.e. the bins aren't emptied regularly; Need to assess the quality of participation and whether communities were willing our unable to participate
What structures and mechanisms were in place which promotes greater or lesser community participation	Why: How is infrastructure procured, is there a role for NGOs in strengthening and facilitating participation of communities in service delivery and O&M. The usual government system of O&M may be reactive – people report their complaints when a service is not working and a response is made. Community participation may make the system more proactive and thus reduce the level of fire fighting. Encourage the local government to represent community interest but intermediaries may be needed to mediate between communities and local government and resolve conflicts. Key sources of information: key informant interviews How: Number of different community organizations and groups, nature of the information flow, variety of decision making process. Comments: is there a role for NGOs and CBOs to facilitate participation; collaboration with communities over technical models, prioritise needs, make most efficient use of limited resources
What methods and tools were used to encourage greater participation?	Why: Methodologies, guidelines, procedures and forms developed to include the communities in planning process, identification of priorities, monitoring services and evaluating them; overcome the barriers to community participation (both within local authorities and communities). O&M workers, officials and NGOs may have different ideas about what makes a good O&M system; workers may focus on resources, officials are concerned with cost recovery and NGOs are interested in institutional issues. Key sources of information: user surveys, key informant interviews How: Number and nature of research and information collection methods Comments: Process are important and not just the products.
What were the roles and responsibility of key stakeholders in O&M	Why: Families may organise some cleaning and maintenance and raise money to hire some paid work; whilst municipalities do major repairs and empty septic tanks. An intermediary organisation may be needed to request assistance from relevant authorities and provide technical advice. Where does the municipality have responsibility to provide O&M for services; what relationship is there between municipalities and line workers Key sources of information: key informants, work logbooks

How clearly were the roles and responsibilities defined?	How: Judge the level of information which is in public domain
	Comments: O&M may be under resources, workers under paid and suffer health risks, poor management and susceptible to political interference
	Why: do community committees exist formally, how are roles and responsibilities defined; signed agreements, designation of O&M roles and responsibilities laid out in agreements, how far is O&M subject to arbitrary factors
	Key sources of information: documentation, work logbooks, key informant interviews, user surveys, rules and regulations in general
	How: Number of incidence where the issues were raised about the roles and responsibilies.
	Comments: role of bribes/ incentives for workers in performing O&M, is O&M provision approached in a comprehensive manner, interaction between municipality and NGOs, not clear what roles and responsibilities the communities have for O&M, the use of quality indicators. NGOs/ CBOs facilitated / supported the stakeholders (communities, munc9ipal, private sector) in providing O&M.

Printed in the USA
CPSIA information can be obtained
at www.ICGtesting.com
JSHW050200160824
68134JS00060B/2621